Allie's Plan

by Ellen Javernick
illustrated by Eric Larsen

Scott Foresman

Editorial Offices: Glenview, Illinois • New York, New York
Sales Offices: Reading, Massachusetts • Duluth, Georgia
Glenview, Illinois • Carrollton, Texas • Menlo Park, California

Allie wanted to shout,

2

Allie covered her nose.
"Sometimes it smells!" she said.

6

"We all have jobs, Allie," said Dad.

"You take out the trash.
Andy walks the dog."

"Working together is what a family is all about."

"Get your job done. Then you can play," said Dad.

"Wait!" said Allie. "I have a great plan!"

"I think this will work," said Dad. "We will make a chart."

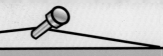

The Chores

	Sun.	Mon.	Tues.	Weds.	Thur.	Fri.	Sat.
Mom	Dishes	Floor	Trash	Dog	Dishes	Floor	Trash
Dad	Floor	Trash	Dog	Dishes	Floor	Trash	Dog
Allie	Trash	Dog	Dishes	Floor	Trash	Dog	Dishes
Andy	Dog	Dishes	Floor	Trash	Dog	Dishes	Floor

Hi!

15